Our Values

CENSORSHIP & PRIVACY

by

Charlie Ogden

Crabtree Publishing Company
www.crabtreebooks.com
1-800-387-7650

Published in Canada
Crabtree Publishing
616 Welland Avenue
St. Catharines, ON
L2M 5V6

Published in the United States
Crabtree Publishing
PMB 59051
350 Fifth Ave, 59th Floor
New York, NY 10118

Published by Crabtree Publishing Company in 2018

First Published by Book Life in 2018
Copyright © 2018 Book Life

Author: Charlie Ogden

Editors: Kirsty Holmes, Janine Deschenes

Design: Danielle Jones

Proofreader: Petrice Custance

**Production coordinator and
  prepress technician (interior):** Margaret Amy Salter

Prepress technician (covers): Ken Wright

Print coordinator: Margaret Amy Salter

Photographs
Abbreviations: l–left, r–right, b–bottom, t–top, c–centre, m–middle.

Front Cover t – By Marcos Mesa Sam Wordley Front Cover b – a katz. 2 – wk1003mike. 4t – ArchMan 4b – Alexander Yakimov. 5 – Vladimir Gjorgiev. 6 – Voronin76. 7 – Syda Productions. 9 – chrisdorney. 10 – See page for author [Public domain], via Wikimedia Commons. 11– Chintung Lee. 12 – Natasa Adzic. 13 – photka. 14 – Vlad Karavaev. 15 – Africa Studio. 16 – GaudiLab. 17 – PR Image Factory. 18 – G_O_S. 19 – REDPIXEL.PL. 20 – alarico. 21 – Georgejmclittle. 22 – http://www.nationalmuseum.af.mil/Upcoming/Photos/igphoto/2000981815/. 23 – Nicku. 24 – Alizada Studios. 25 – Matyas Rehak. 26 – Reporters Sans Frontieres https://rsf.org/sites/default/files/carte_en_2016_.pdf. 27 – Standret. 28 – Forrester Research Inc. http://heatmap.forrestertools.com/. 29 – Richie Chan. 30cr – Maksim Kabakou, 30b – Mert Toker.
Images are courtesy of Shutterstock.com, unless stated otherwise. With thanks to Getty Images, Thinkstock Photo and iStockphoto.

Printed in the USA/012018/BG20171102

Library and Archives Canada Cataloguing in Publication

Ogden, Charlie, author
    Censorship and privacy / Charlie Ogden.

(Our values)
Includes index.
Issued in print and electronic formats.
ISBN 978-0-7787-4731-4 (hardcover).--
ISBN 978-0-7787-4746-8 (softcover).--
ISBN 978-1-4271-2084-7-(HTML)

    1. Freedom of expression--Juvenile literature. 2. Freedom of speech--Juvenile literature. 3. Censorship--Juvenile literature. 4. Mass media--Censorship--Juvenile literature. 5. Privacy, Right of--Juvenile literature. I. Title.

JC585.O33 2018   j323.44   C2017-906925-X
                                             C2017-906926-8

Library of Congress Cataloging-in-Publication Data

CIP available at the Library of Congress

CONTENTS

Words in **bold** can be found in the glossary on page 31.

WHAT IS CENSORSHIP?

We **communicate** with one another constantly, and in many ways—from talking and writing messages, to music, art, and other forms of self-expression. Communicating helps us share our ideas, and learn from the ideas of others. Though communication takes many forms, its purpose is usually the same—to share information with other people so that we can all understand each other and work together.

Censorship is a term used to describe communications that have been blocked, changed, or prohibited. If communication is blocked, that means a person tried to send a message, but it was stopped. If communication is changed, it means that the person's original message was altered before it got to its recipient. If communication is prohibited, it means that the message was not allowed to be sent at all. It can be difficult to know whether communication has been censored or not, because it comes in so many forms.

CENSORSHIP AND FREEDOM OF SPEECH

Censorship attempts to suppress, or take away, a person's freedom of speech. Freedom of speech is the idea that a person should be allowed to express their opinions and thoughts, without being interfered with and without being punished for doing so. According to the **United Nations**, freedom of speech is a **human right**. The right to freedom of speech is upheld in many countries around the world.

However, in some countries, this is not the case. There are many ways a person's freedom of speech can be taken away. Governments can stop freedom of speech by limiting the information that the media, such as news, can share with viewers. Some governments do not allow their citizens to speak against policies in protests. This suppresses freedom of speech. In some places, people are jailed for expressing their opinions.

THE UNIVERSAL DECLARATION OF HUMAN RIGHTS, CREATED BY THE UNITED NATIONS, STATES THAT "EVERYONE HAS THE RIGHT TO FREEDOM OF OPINION AND EXPRESSION [...] AND TO SEE, RECEIVE AND **IMPART** INFORMATION AND IDEAS THROUGH ANY MEDIA."

This is the flag used by the United Nations.

NEWS CENSORSHIP

The news is one of the main places where people receive information from others. Through the news, we can learn about things that have happened in our local **communities**, countries, and around the world. We can also learn information about people, places, and events. Since we get so much of our information from the news, this information informs, or influences, our knowledge about people, places, and events. This means that the way the news presents certain things influences the way we think about them. For example, the words used by the news to describe a person can infuence the way we think about them. Or, if the news describes an event as being successful, we are likely to also think that event was successful.

We know that we rely on the news for information, and the news can influence the way that we think about people, places, and events. That is why censorship of news media is a problem. If the news cannot spread certain information, we may be unable to learn about it at all. Or, if the news is censored in the way that they can present or talk about information, we could be wrongly influenced to think a certain way. News sources can be controlled by people, companies, **organizations,** and even **governments**. Who controls a news source can affect the way news is censored. If a newspaper is controlled by an organization, the organization might censor their news by deleting any **articles** that describe the organization in a negative way. Without negative articles, people might only think of that organization in a positive way.

ART CENSORSHIP

Another place where ideas and expressions are often censored is in art. Art can include a lot of different things. Fine art, such as paintings and drawings, are examples of art. But art also includes music, books, poems, films, and plays. It includes photographs, sculptures, and even clothing.

Art helps us communicate because it allows people to share their thoughts, emotions, and beliefs in different ways. If an artist is feeling a lot of anger, they might paint a picture, play a song, or write a story that expresses that anger. Some artists are able to communicate complicated messages and beliefs through their art, such as their **political** views. Often, art is used to communicate views that are different from mainstream beliefs, or what most people believe.

The messages communicated through art can sometimes make others angry, especially when they go against what many people think or believe. Art may also portray people or things in negative ways. Because of this, art is sometimes censored. However, censoring art takes away a person's freedom of expression, which is their right.

Some governments around the world have censored art, such as music, that communicates political views that go against what the government says.

WHY IS CENSORSHIP AN IMPORTANT ISSUE?

Censorship is an important issue because it can have a huge effect on our lives and the world around us. It can affect the way that we think about things, and our ability to make **informed** choices. It is a powerful tool that can be used by people, organizations, and governments to change the way that people think about the world.

BREAKING

NEWS

Censorship is an important issue because it is often hidden. A lot of the time, people reading censored news don't know that some information has been deleted or changed. They believe what they are reading is the truth—but that is not always the case. We rely on information and messages from others to learn about things and decide how we feel about them. If we are unaware that information or communication has been censored, we are unable to make those decisions.

WHEN CENSORSHIP CAN BE GOOD

There are lots of reasons why censorship is a problem. It can give people the wrong view of the world, it can stop beautiful and important art from being viewed or experienced worldwide, and—importantly—it takes away a person's right to freedom of speech, opinion, and expression. However, sometimes censorship can protect people.

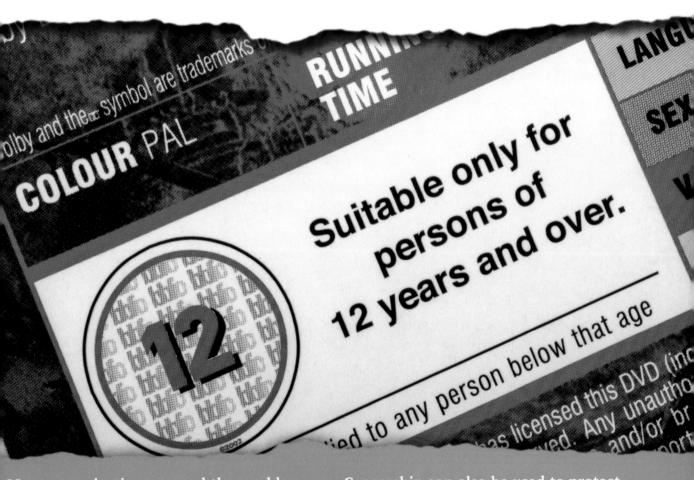

Many organizations around the world censor news and art so that they are okay to be viewed by children. They might change words or delete aspects of the information or art that can't be properly understood by children. This mostly happens in films, television shows, and songs on the radio. The organizations that censor bad language or violence from a film do so to protect children.

Censorship can also be used to protect people who are at risk. Most news organizations do not print the names of some victims of crimes. This is to protect their privacy. Many news organizations also censor the names of the people who provide them with information. They do this because in some cases, people are punished for telling the media information. For example, a person giving information about wrongful practices at their workplace could be fired if the media did not censor their name.

WHEN CENSORSHIP CAN BE BAD

While censorship can sometimes help people, in most cases it is used to control the type of information people receive, making them think a certain way. Governments have been known to use censorship in many different ways to affect the thoughts of their **citizens**. Censoring certain information can help a government stay in power or maintain control over its citizens.

Governments sometimes censor news, art, and other media so that they agree with the views of the government. This is very dangerous, especially in countries that have governments with very strict ideas on what people are allowed to do or say. There, censoring news and art is a way for governments to make many people agree with these strict ideas.

ANIMAL FARM

A FAIRY STORY

by

GEORGE ORWELL

THE BOOK *ANIMAL FARM* BY GEORGE ORWELL WAS BANNED IN MANY COUNTRIES FOR A LONG TIME BECAUSE IT CRITICIZED, OR SPOKE NEGATIVELY ABOUT, A TYPE OF GOVERNMENT. IT IS STILL BANNED IN SOME COUNTRIES TODAY.

Some governments take censorship further and choose all of the news and art that is available to their citizens. They control all forms of news, media, and art in their country, including newspapers, television news, films and television shows, and information on the Internet. In cases like this, the government often creates news information, art, and other media itself. Often, news, art, and media that comes from outside the country is not allowed to be viewed there. When people only get their information from one source—their government—they are forced to learn only those views.

This is Pyongyang, the capital city of North Korea.

One country known for censoring its news, art, and media is North Korea. The North Korean government often censors news, so that North Korean citizens only see positive news about the government. Television news in North Korea often reports that North Korea is a strong and powerful country, where people are very happy. In reality, many people in North Korea are very poor and do not have enough food to eat. The country's citizens also do not have a lot of freedom.

WHAT IS PRIVACY?

Privacy can mean a lot of different things. At its core, it is the idea that a person can be free from the public attention of others. Privacy can refer to not having to share some things with others—from personal information to thoughts and feelings. Privacy can also refer to the ability to make decisions about private matters or engage in private activities without outside regulation, intrusion, or influence. This can sometimes include government regulations on activities.

It is really important to **respect** the privacy of others. There are many countries around the world, including the United States and Canada, that have laws that protect people's privacy.

PRIVACY AND INFORMATION

When it comes to our personal information, privacy is really important. In the digital world we live in, personal information could be easily accessed online—making it not-so-private. This can be dangerous. If the wrong people have our private information, they can use it in negative ways. For example, we keep information about our money safe and private, so no one can steal our money using this information. We also keep things like our address, age, and medical information private. This information is only for you, and most other people do not need to know it. It's important to be careful with the information we put online.

The United States and Canadian governments both have laws that work to protect the privacy of a person's personal information. These laws require any organization that collects personal information, such as a workplace or health organization, to keep the information private.

Physical privacy is another type of privacy that is important to people. It refers to the desire to keep one's body private from other people. Wearing clothing and using private bathrooms and showers are some ways people keep their bodies private. It is very important to respect others' physical privacy.

PRIVACY AND CULTURE

Privacy affects every person on Earth. There are things that every person wants to keep private. Some of these things are kept private for one's safety, such as personal information. But other views on privacy are based on one's personal beliefs and culture. The ways that people think about privacy often depend on their culture. The things that people choose to keep private can change a lot between different cultures. For example, in many cultures around the world, physical privacy is important. People cover parts of their bodies that they don't want others to see. However in other cultures, physical privacy is not important. In some **tribes** in Africa, for example, nudity is normal.

Despite different cultural views on privacy, it is a human right. According to the United Nations' Universal Declaration of Human Rights, "No one shall be subjected to arbitrary interference with his privacy, family, home, or correspondence."

If something is arbitrary, it means a person chose to do it without the consent of others. The Declaration also states that if one's privacy is violated in these ways, they have the right to protection by privacy laws.

LIMITS OF PRIVACY

Although privacy is a human right, according to the United Nations, and many countries have laws protecting privacy, there are circumstances where privacy is limited. This means that there are some things that people cannot keep private, no matter how much they want to. Usually, this refers to personal information that governments or organizations need—or want—in order to do their jobs.

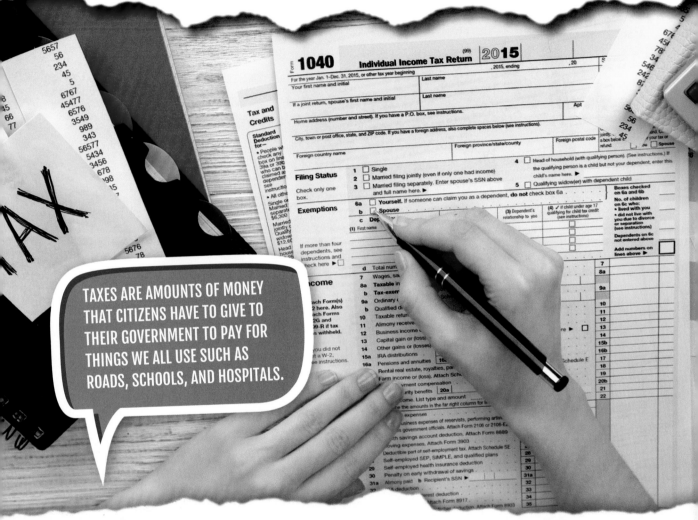

TAXES ARE AMOUNTS OF MONEY THAT CITIZENS HAVE TO GIVE TO THEIR GOVERNMENT TO PAY FOR THINGS WE ALL USE SUCH AS ROADS, SCHOOLS, AND HOSPITALS.

Governments often make **laws** about what information has to be shared with the government. For example, people in most countries have to tell the government how much money they make. This is so that the government can take the right amount of taxes from each citizen. Governments also may collect personal communications for security reasons, to make sure no one is planning harm to others. In other cases, companies collect personal information to learn more about their potential customers. They might collect your search history online, for example, to see which products you are interested in. Some people feel that these are **unethical** invasions of privacy.

WHY IS PRIVACY IMPORTANT?

It is very important to understand when to respect the human right of privacy. It is also important to know that privacy has limits. However, ideas about privacy change between different people, between different cultures, and between governments. It can be difficult to decide which information needs to be shared with governments and organizations, and which information should be kept private. For example, some people are okay with their government accessing private communications if it is part of keeping the country safe. Others disagree.

Some information needs to be shared. To pay your cell phone bill, you need to share your billing address, and credit card or bank account number. However, not all situations are as clear as this one. There is a lot of personal information that doesn't need to be shared—but is shared anyway. If this information doesn't need to be shared, most people agree that it should be up to the individual whether they share it or not. If a person does not want to share this information, then no one should force them to.

Talking about privacy is very important because the limits of privacy are not always clear. When is it okay for someone to be made to share information about themselves and when would this be wrong?

Forcing people to share their personal information can sometimes help people. However, many people believe that a person's right to privacy shouldn't be taken away, under any circumstances.

Another reason why privacy is so important today is that **technology** is making it easier for people to share—and steal—information. New technology has led to new questions about privacy. We know that when people share things online with others, they are no longer private. But there are also companies that ask for, or gather, personal information online. What happens when these companies are hacked, or when they do not follow practices to keep information safe? Are advances in technology creating more privacy problems?

COMPANIES WHO HANDLE OUR PRIVATE INFORMATION, SUCH AS CREDIT CARD INFORMATION WHEN WE DO ONLINE SHOPPING, HAVE TO LOOK AFTER THAT INFORMATION AND KEEP IT SAFE. THIS IS CALLED DATA PROTECTION, AND IS THE LAW IN MOST COUNTRIES.

CENSORSHIP AND PRIVACY

It is important to think about the connection between censorship and privacy. Censorship is one way that information can be kept private. Personal information can be censored to keep it private, or being seen or used by others. Media can be censored to protect children from seeing inappropriate content. But censorship can also be used to keep information private from the public, so that their opinions or knowledge is swayed. It is important to think about the connection between censorship and privacy.

Privacy and censorship in the media are especially important in today's world because so many people use the Internet and television to get information. When should censorship be used to keep information private from the media?

CENSORSHIP AND PRIVACY IN THE MEDIA

Sometimes, it is important to censor personal information in the media. People's information should not be spread widely on television or the Internet. We often put our personal information on the Internet when we use **social media** websites. These websites are a great way to connect with others, but we all need to be careful about sharing information about ourselves. Once information has been shared online, it is very difficult to make it private again.

DON'T PUT PERSONAL INFORMATION ON SOCIAL MEDIA SITES. THIS INCLUDES YOUR FULL NAME, YOUR ADDRESS OR TELEPHONE NUMBER, WHAT SCHOOL YOU GO TO, OR ANYTHING ELSE YOU WOULDN'T WANT STRANGERS TO KNOW.

Some people, especially famous people and celebrities, have their personal information posted all over the Internet. These people sometimes do not want their information to be shared. Often, personal information and photographs of them are shared without their consent.

Many celebrities make money as a public figure, so some people think it is okay to share their personal information. Others think that celebrities, even if they are in the public eye, deserve privacy too. It can be unsafe for the media to share their personal information, such as their address. What do you think?

CENSORSHIP AND PRIVACY IN THE MEDIA

Though censorship in the media can be used to keep personal information private, censoring media information often results in negative effects. Most countries are affected by censorship in the media in some way.

Equatorial Guinea

This is Bata, the largest city in Equatorial Guinea.

The radio news in Equatorial Guinea is heavily censored to make people believe in what the president and his government are doing. Any **criticisms** of the president, his family, or his government are banned from being put on the main media—radio. This makes it harder for negative views about the president to become wide spread in the country. In this way, censorship is used in the media to keep certain opinions from being shared.

Some **media outlets** censor information by sharing something known as fake news. Fake news stories are articles that look like they are true, but are partially or completely false. Fake news stories can manipulate, or change, true information in order to influence the way readers or viewers feel about a subject. Fake news is a type of censorship because it stops true information from being shared. Because of this, people getting their news from the television or the Internet can find it difficult to know whether the information they are reading or hearing about is true.

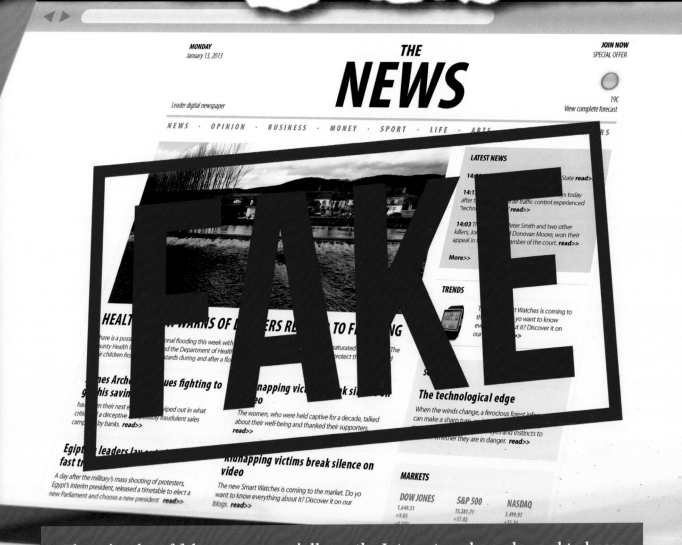

There is a lot of fake news, especially on the Internet, and people need to know that not everything they read online is true. Luckily, some companies and websites, such as Facebook, are providing tips and strategies to help people know the difference between a fake news article and one that is true. For example, readers should always look closely at the website **URL** and examine the sources that are used to support a story.

CENSORSHIP AND PRIVACY
IN HISTORY

WORLD WAR ONE

During World War One, thousands of letters were being sent between soldiers and their families back home every day. These letters were important for keeping the soldiers' **morale** up, and also for helping the family members at home know the soldiers were alive. However, there was a problem. Enemy armies might see the letters. If the letters contained information about the soldiers' plans, the enemy armies could use that information to win battles or harm the soldiers.

ugene Dudley was the most

elpful. Finally from

Even mention of the weather was censored from soldiers' letters during World War One.

on July 27 an offic

office from the gov However we

In order to make sure that the letters being sent to and from the soldiers in World War One did not contain any information that could help the enemy, they were censored by officers in the army. Forbidden information included any mention of the location of soldiers or the number of soldiers in each of the **trenches**. Censoring letters meant that soldiers could still write to their loved ones without putting the success of the war at risk.

RELIGIOUS CENSORSHIP

Religious censorship is when a religious organization, such as a church, blocks information from being shared. Usually, information that goes against the organization's religious beliefs is censored. There is a long history of religious censorship, and it has occurred in almost every major religion and **civilization** in history. Many governments in past civilizations were closely linked to religion, which gave religious organizations in the past a lot of power to censor information.

Nicolaus Copernicus

Nicolaus Copernicus published a book in 1543 that explained how objects in the solar system **orbit** one another. Up until then, people believed that Earth was the center of the **Solar System** and that the Sun, Moon, and other planets all orbited around it. This view was accepted by the **Catholic Church** because it believed Earth was created by God—making it the most important planet.

Copernicus created a scientific model that argued that that the Sun, not Earth, was at the center of the Solar System and that the planets all orbited around it. Today, we know that Copernicus was correct. At the time, however, his ideas were rejected by the Catholic Church. This made it difficult for his scientific research to become widely-known until many years after his death.

THE STASI

After World War Two ended in 1945, Germany was divided and its parts were controlled by the United States, France, Britain, and the **Soviet Union**. It was eventually split into two parts—East Germany and West Germany. East Germany, controlled by the Soviet Union, was run by a very controlling government that used a large and powerful secret police force called the Stasi. Its main job was to spy on the people of East Germany to make sure they supported the government, and were not cooperating with the opposing government of West Germany.

This museum in Leipzig, Germany, displays different items that were used by the Stasi to spy on people.

One way that the Stasi spied on the citizens of East Germany was by using informants. Informants were people who pretended to be normal citizens. When they found out any useful information, they passed it on to the Stasi. This information was usually about their family, friends, or co-workers. It was difficult for people to know who to trust. The Stasi also used **surveillance** technology, such as hidden cameras and hidden microphones, to spy on the citizens of East Germany. Each of these methods secretly invaded citizens' privacy.

People who were seen to go against the East German government were often arrested and threatened by the Stasi until they told them names of other people who did not agree with the East German government. When the East German government was overthrown in 1990, the world became fully aware of what the Stasi had done. There were thousands of files containing detailed notes about almost every single person living in East Berlin—the capital city of East Germany.

This building in Berlin, Germany, was used as a prison by the Stasi.

Today, some of the Stasi files are open to the public. This allows us to study the history of the Stasi and learn about what happened. However, files that contain personal information about the people who used to live in East Germany have not been released. They are tightly controlled to protect the privacy of the people.

CENSORSHIP AND PRIVACY TODAY

Censorship and privacy are still important issues today. There are many places around the world where censorship is over-used and privacy is not respected.

Below is a map that shows how free the media is in different countries around the world. A free media means that it is not controlled or censored by outside influences, such as governments and organizations. The map shows how much censorship is used by organizations and governments in different countries.

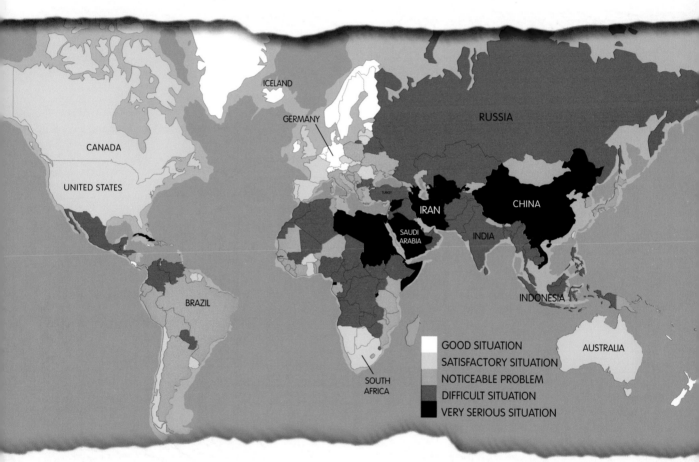

ICELAND
GERMANY
RUSSIA
CANADA
UNITED STATES
TURKEY
IRAN
CHINA
SAUDI ARABIA
INDIA
BRAZIL
INDONESIA
AUSTRALIA
SOUTH AFRICA

GOOD SITUATION
SATISFACTORY SITUATION
NOTICEABLE PROBLEM
DIFFICULT SITUATION
VERY SERIOUS SITUATION

Using the key, we can see that there are very few places in the world that are in a "Good Situation"—in which the amount of censorship of their media is very small. Two countries that are marked on the map as being in a "Very Serious Situation" are Saudi Arabia and Iran. These two countries are still controlled by religious laws. In these countries, all the news outlets are censored to make sure they agree with these laws. Any opinions that go against the religious beliefs in the country may be blocked. In some cases, people who disagree with the religious laws might be put in prison.

One country that ranks very highly on the map, meaning that there is a very low level of censorship in the country, is the Netherlands. The freedom of the media in the Netherlands is heavily protected by the law, making it very difficult for a news outlet to censor any news.

As long as an article isn't hateful or unfair towards one group of people, there is very little that is banned from the news in the Netherlands. Because of this, everyone's right to freedom of speech is well protected in the country.

This is Amsterdam, the capital city of the Netherlands.

Many of the countries that have free media have something in common—they all have laws in place that stop organizations and the government from censoring news unless it is harmful or untrue. Putting similar laws in place in other countries could help reduce censorship there.

Below is a map that shows how different countries compare in terms of their privacy laws. The countries in blue have many laws in place to protect the privacy of their citizens. The countries in red have very few laws or no laws protecting their citizens' privacy. The map shows that in many countries, there are few laws that protect citizens' privacy. The gray areas note countries where there was no information found about privacy laws.

Most restricted
Restricted
Some restrictions
Minimal restrictions
Effectively no restrictions
No legislation or no information
Government surveillance may impact privacy

This map also shows countries where the government is using surveillance. Surveillance is the close, ongoing watch over someone to collect information about their activities. Although many countries have some laws to protect privacy, the map shows that many of them—including the United States and the United Kingdom—use surveillance to spy on and collect information about the citizens in their country.

In June 2013, multiple media sources broke the story that the National Security Agency (NSA) in the United States was collecting private telephone records of American citizens. The source of the story was Edward Snowden, a former NSA employee.

OPINIONS ABOUT SNOWDEN ARE MIXED. SOME PEOPLE SEE HIM AS A TRAITOR AGAINST THE UNITED STATES. OTHERS BELIEVE HE IS A HERO FOR EXPOSING THE GOVERNMENT'S VIOLATION OF PERSONAL PRIVACY.

In this image, Snowden supporters protest against government surveillance in Washington, D.C.

STOP MASS SPYING

stopwatching.us

We the People Oppose the Surveillance State and say: THANK YOU, EDWARD SNOWDEN!

STOP MASS SPYING

stopwatching.us

Snowden wanted the American people to know that the government was watching and collecting their personal communications. He felt that it was wrong for the government to invade the privacy of the country's citizens. However, the NSA stated that Snowden's actions had caused harm to the security of the United States. The US government stated that their surveillance operations were used only for national security reasons, and were necessary to protect citizens of the United States. Today, Snowden lives in Russia. If he returns to the United States, he will be arrested and charged with crimes.

THINK ABOUT IT!

Ideas about censorship and privacy are complicated. Use these prompts to discuss your ideas with friends and classmates.

 1 What information about a person do you think should be kept private?

 2 When do you think censorship is okay? When do you think it is wrong?

3 Are there any times when a person should not have freedom of speech?

GLOSSARY

articles — A piece of writing about a topic that is included with others in a publication

Catholic Church — A branch of Christianity led by the Pope

citizens — People who live in a specific town, city, or country

civilization — An advanced human society

communicate — To exchange information with others

community — A group of people who live, work, and play in a place

criticisms — The disapproval of something based on its flaws or problems

governments — The group of people who control a country and make its laws

human right — A right that is believed to belong to every person, because they are human

impart — To share information or communicate

informed — Having or sharing knowledge about a subject

laws — Rules made by government that everyone in a country must follow

media outlet — A company or organization that produces media, such as radio, television, and the Internet

morale — The confidence and enthusiasm of a person or group at a particular time

orbit — The path that an object makes around a larger object in space

organizations — Groups of people with a particular purpose, such as businesses or charities

political — Relating to the government of a country and its affairs and activities

respect — Recognize the importance of

social media — Websites and applications that allow people to communicate and connect with each other

Solar System — The eight planets, including Earth, that orbit around the Sun, along with other space bodies such as moons and asteroids

Soviet Union — A former federation that existed from 1922 to 1991, created after the Russian Revolution

surveillance — The close observation of a person, often using technology

technology — Machines or devices that are made using scientific knowledge

trenches — Long ditches in the ground used to shield soldiers, common during World War One

tribe — A group of people linked by a common culture

unethical — Morally wrong; not following principles of right and wrong

United Nations — An organization of many nations started in 1945 to promote world peace

INDEX